READING POWER

Record-Breaking Structures

The Maracana
World's Largest Soccer Stadium

Mark Thomas

The Rosen Publishing Group's
PowerKids Press™
New York

Published in 2002 by The Rosen Publishing Group, Inc.
29 East 21st Street, New York, NY 10010

Copyright © 2002 by The Rosen Publishing Group, Inc.

All rights reserved. No part of this book may be reproduced in any form without permission in writing from the publisher, except by a reviewer.

First Edition

Book Design: Sam Jordan

Photo Credits: Cover, pp. 4–6 © Yann Arthus-Bertrand/Corbis; pp. 8, 10–11, 20 © J.L. Bulkao/Gamma; p. 9 © Archive Photo; p.12 © Corbis; pp. 13, 18–19 © The Image Works; pp. 15, 21 © AP/Wide World Photos; pp. 16–17 © Roberto Gomez/Gamma; p. 19 (inset) © Dennis O'Regan/Corbis.

Thomas, Mark.
The Maracana : world's largest soccer stadium / Mark Thomas.
   p. cm. — (Record-breaking structures)
Includes bibliographical references and index.
ISBN 0-8239-5992-9 (library binding)
1. Estâadio do Maracanäa (Rio de Janeiro, Brazil)—Juvenile literature. [1. Maracanäa Stadium (Rio de Janeiro, Brazil) 2. Stadiums—Brazil.] I. Title.
TH4714 .T49 2001
725'.827'098153—dc21
                                      2001000598

Manufactured in the United States of America

Contents

World's Largest Soccer Stadium	4
Location	6
Building the Stadium	8
Fun and Games	12
Record-Breaking Crowds	16
Glossary	22
Resources	23
Index	24
Word Count	24
Note	24

World's Largest Soccer Stadium

The Maracana Stadium was built in 1950 as the world's largest soccer stadium. It was made to hold 200,000 people.

Location

The Maracana Stadium is in Rio de Janeiro. Rio de Janeiro is the second-largest city in Brazil. Brazil is a country in South America.

Building the Stadium

The stadium is shaped like an oval bowl.

There are two main levels where people can sit.

The stadium was built with cement and iron. More than 500,000 bags of cement were used. Over 10,000 tons of iron were used, too.

Fun and Games

Soccer is very important to the people of Brazil. They love watching their favorite players. Many of the top soccer players, like Pelé, become heroes to the fans.

Pelé

A soccer game at the Maracana is like a big party. The fans make a lot of noise. They love cheering for their favorite teams.

Record-Breaking Crowds

Many fans go to every soccer game at the Maracana. In 1950, 199,854 people went to see a game. This is still a record for the most people ever at a soccer game.

Many people go to the Maracana to see concerts. On April 20, 1990, 184,000 people went to see singer Paul McCartney. This is a record for the most people ever at a concert in a stadium.

Paul McCartney

The world's best soccer players and entertainers play at the Maracana. Many tourists also visit the stadium.

The people of Brazil are very proud of their record-breaking stadium.

Glossary

Brazil (bruh-**zihl**) a country in South America

cement (suh-**mehnt**) gray powder that is mixed with water to make concrete

entertainers (ehn-tuhr-**tay**-nuhrz) people who perform in public

Maracana Stadium (ma-ra-**ka**-nuh **stay**-dee-uhm) the world's largest soccer arena ever built where people go to watch sports or concerts

oval (**oh**-vuhl) shaped like an egg

record (**rehk**-uhrd) the highest score, amount, or speed ever reached

Rio de Janeiro (**ree**-oh **day** zhuh-**nehr**-oh) the second largest city in Brazil

tourists (**tur**-ihsts) people who enjoy traveling

Resources

Books

Building Big
by David Macaulay
Houghton Mifflin Company (2000)

America's Top 10 Construction Wonders
by Tanya Lee Stone
Blackbirch Press (1998)

Web Site

http://www.triumphbusiness.com/tourism/maracana.htm

Index

B
Brazil, 6–7, 12, 21

C
cement, 10

E
entertainers, 20

F
fans, 12, 14, 16

M
McCartney, Paul, 18–19

P
Pelé, 12

R
record, 16, 18
Rio de Janeiro, 6–7

S
South America, 6

T
teams, 14
tourists, 20

Word Count: 235

Note to Librarians, Teachers, and Parents

If reading is a challenge, Reading Power is a solution! Reading Power is perfect for readers who want high-interest subject matter at an accessible reading level. These fact-filled, photo-illustrated books are designed for readers who want straightforward vocabulary, engaging topics, and a manageable reading experience. With clear picture/text correspondence, leveled Reading Power books put the reader in charge. Now readers have the power to get the information they want and the skills they need in a user-friendly format.